LOVING THE CHURCH

SCRIPTURAL MEDITATIONS
FOR THE PAPAL HOUSEHOLD

Loving the Church

RANIERO CANTALAMESSA, O.F.M., Cap.

*Translated by Gilberto Cavazos-González, O.F.M.
and Amanda Quantz*

SERVANT
BOOKS

PUBLISHED BY ST. ANTHONY MESSENGER PRESS
CINCINNATI, OHIO

Loving the Church was published originally as *Amare la Chiesa: Meditazioni sulla Lettera agli Efesini*, copyright 2003 by Ancora Editrice, Italy.

Cover design by Candle Light Studios
Book design by Phillips Robinette, O.F.M.

Library of Congress Cataloging-in-Publication Data

Cantalamessa, Raniero.
  [Amare la chiesa. English]
  Loving the church : Scriptural meditations for the Papal household /
Raniero Cantalamessa ; translated by Gilberto Cavazos and Amanda Quantz.
    p. cm.
  ISBN 0-86716-637-1 (alk. paper)
  1. Bible. N.T. Ephesians—Meditations. 2. Church—Biblical teaching—
Meditations. 3. Catholic Church—Doctrines—Meditations. I. Title.
  BS2695.6.C5C36 2005
  262—dc22
                              2004027378

ISBN 0-86716-637-1
Copyright 2003 by Ancora S.r.l.
English translation copyright ©2005, St. Anthony Messenger Press

Published by Servant Books, an imprint of St. Anthony Messenger Press
www. AmericanCatholic.org
Printed in the United States of America

05 06 07 08 09 5 4 3 2 1

Table of Contents

Lectio Divina

This short volume contains four reflections of *lectio divina* that I gave to the papal household during Lent of 2003. The final chapter was offered to a different audience and concerns the family as the "domestic Church."

The main characteristic of *lectio divina*, as compared to other forms of meditation, is that its foundation is Scripture. Here Scripture does not serve as an example, nor does it function as a part of the meditation in order to illustrate a given theme. Rather, Scripture itself constitutes the theme from which everything begins and to which everything returns.

Another noteworthy characteristic of *lectio divina* is that it is usually a continuous reading of a particular book of the Bible. Both of these characteristics are visible in the reflections in this volume. Each is based on an excerpt from the Letter to the Ephesians, and the reflections follow the order in which the excerpts appear in Scripture.

As always with reflections given to the papal household, the first part provides some essential theological considerations about the issue at hand. The second part then presents the practical implications for the spiritual life that spring forth from those considerations. Some of these practical applications, such as those in Chapter Three on the spirituality of service to the Chair of Peter, are meant for the audience to which they were originally addressed. I keep them in the book since indirectly they may interest everyone.

Following the progression in Ephesians, we contemplate the Church under the four classical images of building, body, bride and mother.

In Chapter Four, I make an observation concerning the necessity and urgency of new reflections on the mystery of the Church:

> It was predicted at the beginning of the twentieth century that that would be the century of the Church, the century in which the Church would become newly aware of its importance after the long silence of the liberal enlightenment period. This certainly happened at the theological level. There were countless studies on the nature of the Church. Karl Barth called his study *Church Dogmatics*. The Second Vatican Council made his work a focal point. There was also the *Ecclesiam suam* of Paul VI. But did love for the Church grow proportionately?

One cannot read the affirmation of Ephesians 5:25, "Christ loved the Church," without asking the question, "And I? Do I love the Church?"

CHAPTER ONE

"Through Him the Whole Structure Is Held Together"

$\mathcal{I}$n the latter part of *Novo millennio ineunte*, the Pope invites us to consider the "mystery of the Church" as a communion that has charity at its heart.[1] It is in this spirit that we wish to reread some excerpts from the Letter to the Ephesians, the ecclesiological text *par excellence* of all the New Testament. The Letter to the Ephesians speaks of universal reconciliation, of enmity destroyed, of dividing walls torn down. We are constrained to read this letter at a time in which we are surrounded by "rumors of war" and enmity among former friends, which seems to triumph around the planet. This is a time when we need to rehear the words "Christ is our peace." The Letter to the Ephesians states: "He came and proclaimed peace to you who were far off and peace to those who were near" (Eph 2:14, 17). These are words that the world needs to hear again and again.

Let us dedicate ourselves to hearing God's word, for "whatever was written in former days was written for our instruction, so that by steadfastness and by the encouragement of the scriptures we might have hope" (Rom 15:4).

A Dangerous Letter?

It is no longer thought that the Letter to the Ephesians comes from the hand of St. Paul. It comes from a period just after the apostle, from someone who gathered and developed his thought. This, however, is of relatively little interest to us. Knowing that Ephesians is part of the canon of the inspired Scriptures is enough to assure us that God speaks through it with all of his divine authority.

How is the Church presented in Ephesians? The most relevant novelty is, without a doubt, that up to now Paul used the word *church* to speak exclusively about the local church (Jerusalem, Corinth, Philippi, and so on), but here and in the Letter to the Colossians it is used to indicate the universal Church—universal not just in space but also in time, inasmuch as it has its origins in God before time began. The Church is both celestial and earthly.

Some have seen in this novelty the danger of excessive ecclesiological enthusiasm and triumphalism. A well-known commentator wrote recently:

> From the theological point of view, the image of the Church draws precariously close to that of a glorious community that resides more in heaven than on earth, bound to its triumphant Lord. The Church, on the other hand, is rarely seen at the foot of the cross, in the *sequela* (following) of the Lord who suffers and dies. This perspective is more prevalent today than it was in previous centuries. In my understanding this constitutes a danger for our ecclesial consciousness.[2]

If this is a fault, I say that it is for us "a happy fault," a providential fault. We are more inclined to see the dark side of the Church than to have a positive vision of it, which is truly the corrective that we need at this moment. In reference to the well-known definition of the Church as "chaste whore" (*casta meretrix*) the noun *whore* has so often been insisted upon that we have developed a longing to hear something about the adjective *chaste*.[3]

Further, we will see that the danger mentioned is more imaginary than real. Far from indulging in quietist attitudes of self-aggrandizement, the Letter to the Ephesians is a continual exhortation to change, to seek interior renewal. Mystery is not called upon except to make it the norm of life. The cross is not absent, because in it, our letter says, enmity has been destroyed and the great reconciliation is accomplished (see Eph 2:16).

No Longer Strangers

The first topic of our reflection is in Ephesians 2:19-22. In keeping with the method of *lectio divina*, we would like first of all to listen to the original text:

> So then you are no longer strangers and aliens, but you are citizens with the saints and also members of the household of God, built upon the foundation of the apostles and prophets, with Christ Jesus himself as the cornerstone. In him the whole structure is joined together and grows into a holy temple in the Lord; in whom you also are built together spiritually into a dwelling place for God.

Here the Church is presented to us with the guiding images of edifice and the process of construction. It is not just any structure; but rather, it is the sacred edifice *par excellence*, the temple and the dwelling place of God. It is significant that the word *church* has always embraced both meanings: that of a material edifice and that of a spiritual reality, the people of God.

The Letter to the Ephesians is not the only letter to use construction imagery in reference to the Church. Paul defines the believers as "God's field, God's building" (1 Cor 3:9), and the First Letter of Peter calls them "living stones,...built into a spiritual house" (1 Pt 2:5). The final phrase of our text, "built together, spiritually into a

9

dwelling place for God," recalls the Pauline concept that every believer is "God's temple" and that "God's Spirit dwells" in each one (1 Cor 3:16).

The hymn of blessing with which the letter begins names the three "architects" who designed and, each in his own time, realized this project. They are the Father, who conceived the design before the creation of the world; Jesus Christ, who realized it in the fullness of time; and the Holy Spirit, who placed his seal upon it. Christ is the "cornerstone" of the edifice or, according to another interpretation, the "keystone" that crowns the building. The apostles and prophets are the foundation; not as of themselves, but because through them one arrives at the only foundation, who is Christ (see 1 Cor 3:11).

There was a time when, following the influential studies of H. Schlier, they read the Letter to the Ephesians in an anti-gnostic key, as the Christian answer to the need to provide a heavenly basis for an earthly reality. Already in our text we find an initial rejection of this theory—a theory that in any event everyone has by now abandoned. The term *construction* has either the passive meaning of a constructed edifice or the active meaning of the construction of the edifice. The Church therefore is built in time; it is not a preexistent reality having its life only in heaven. Its celestial preexistence is only intentional (in the mind of God), while its earthly existence as well as its future eschatological existence are real.

The Wall Destroyed

According to Gregory the Great, Scripture *crescit cum legentibus*[4] ("grows with those who read it"). It always gives new answers as new questions confront it. This is true of the Letter to the Ephesians. Chapter two, the topic of this reflection, has much to say to modern society.

At the margins of the dialogue between Jews and Christians are ideas that are in direct conflict with the teachings of our letter. Ephesians states that Christ "has made both groups into one," that he "has broken down the dividing wall" that was between them, so that he might "reconcile both groups to God in one body'" (Eph 2:14, 16). Today, with the best of intentions, some would like to rebuild the wall that Christ has torn down, so as to have not one but two edifices, separate and independent of each other.[5]

The Church has recognized in various documents the permanent value of the old covenant as well as its salvific character for those who, in good conscience, live according to it. Some think that the Church is saying that the Jews can do without Christ and that the mission of the Church is directed to the gentiles. They support their argument by the fact that in his missionary mandate, Jesus ordered the apostles to "make disciples of all nations" (Mt 28:19), referring to the pagan peoples. They apply to the relationship between Israel and the Church what Paul says of Peter and himself with regard to their roles: One is for the circumcised and the other for the uncircumcised (see Gal 2:7-8).

This removes from Christians not only a direct missionary commitment to the Jews but even the desire and the hope that someday they, too, will come to know Christ. I read in a reputable Catholic magazine:

> But, many Jews would say, though the Church has abandoned any formal attempts to convert Jews, and

understands itself to be "with" and not "over against" the Jews, don't Catholics still in their hearts long for their conversion? Might not that longing, frustrated, pop out again one day as it has so often over the centuries?[6]

To this the author responded that this could be true of some isolated Catholics but not of the Church in general. The Church has renounced, according to him, even praying for the conversion of the Jews. He contended that even though it is true the Good Friday liturgy prays that the Jews "may arrive at the fullness of redemption," by this we do not mean redemption in Christ but the final, eschatological one.[7]

If this were so, then I would declare myself one of those "isolated Catholics." I desire that our Jewish brothers and sisters, whom I love, will one day come to know him whom Simeon called "a light for revelation to the Gentiles and for glory to your people Israel" (Lk 2:32). May they come, not forced nor even solicited by us, but rather autonomously, through their own discovery, within their own faith, losing nothing of their identity as "Israel according to the flesh." To renounce even the desire of this is, for me, not to love either Christ or the Jews.

Mission to Israel

It is absurd and contrary to the entire New Testament to think that the mission of Christ is directed to the pagans and not to the Jews, when all of Christ's preaching and his call to conversion is directed to the Jews, and he himself says that he came for the lost sheep of the house of Israel (see Mt 15:24; see also Acts 13:46). The idea according to which Jesus is the Messiah of the gentiles, the *goyim*, but not of the Jewish people was the position of some Jewish theologians of the twentieth century (Rosenzweig, Schoeps, Herberg), worthy as such of every consideration, but Christian theology and the Vatican II never made it their own.

The mistake is born of a false interpretation of the significance of conversion. On the lips of Jesus—clearly stated in Mark 1:15—"conversion" did not mean the passage from idolatry to the cult of the true God, nor did it mean to renounce something; it simply meant "to believe in the gospel." It did not mean to turn back but rather to take a step forward and enter into the reign that has come. "For I am not ashamed of the gospel," writes the apostle to the gentiles. "It is the power of God for salvation to everyone who has faith, to the Jew first and also to the Greek" (Rom 1:16).

We need to be attentive, surely, to not put the acceptance of Jesus of Nazareth on the same level as the acceptance of that which was born of him and developed by him throughout the centuries—that is to say, Christianity. While it is true that Christ and the Church cannot be separated, neither can they be confused with each other. It is not because of the word of the Church that Jesus is accepted, but more accurately it is because of the word of Jesus that the Church is accepted. We need a gradual process of education when it comes to the Jewish people, who have suffered so much at the hands of Christians and the Church.

With regard to the Jews, the only possible attitude is to take literally the Letter of Peter: "Be ready to make your defense to anyone who demands from you an accounting for the hope that is in you" (1 Pt 3:15). That is, we must not take on the initiatives of evangelization on our own, but when the occasion arises we are to give witness to the hope that Christ is for us. Peter says, "with gentleness and reverence," and we add, "and in a spirit of sincere repentance for the past." No need to fear that in this line one ends up wishing the end of the Hebrew religion with its unique heritage. We Christians must take into account what Jesus said, "Do not think that I have come to abolish the law or the prophets; I have come not to abolish but to fulfill" (Mt 5:17). I am convinced that the conversion of Israel to the Church (if there should be one) will at the same time be a conversion of the Church to Israel.

I was moved by the concerned comment of a Jewish convert on the question of the risk of seeing the gospel withheld, not only in fact but also in principle from the people of her race.

> Israel's lack of belief is not so great a mystery to me as my belief.... But to deny that it is Christ alone who saves, that the Old Covenant was, as Paul says, "our schoolmaster to lead us to Christ" (Gal 3:24, *NASB*), the one mediator between God and men (1 Tm 2:5), is to deny Christ for ourselves. If he is not the Messiah of Israel—God come in the flesh (1 Jn 4:2)—then he is no one's Messiah.... Growing up in a conservative Jewish home in Brooklyn, New York, I experienced considerable amounts of anti-Semitism, often from Catholics through whom, though I did not understand so at the time, the face of Christ was disfigured. It is not difficult for me to understand the reluctance—or, perhaps more accurately, the aversion—that most Jews have to hearing the gospel. Yet God, in his infinite grace and mercy, reached out to each member of my immediate family, my parents included, and not only brought us through those experiences but into the Church—and

> thereby into communion with the very people, though few, whose anti-Semitism had caused us such travail.[8]

Her affirmation "If he is not the Messiah of Israel then he is no one's Messiah" really struck me because of its obvious truth. "Messiah" is in fact what he has claimed to be. The Letter to the Ephesians seems to have been written as a response in anticipation of the contemporary problem that assails us, a just relationship with Israel. Of all the writings of the New Testament, this Letter is probably the one that expresses itself most positively and with greatest respect with regard to the Jews. Its central message is that "the Gentiles have become fellow heirs (with Israel), members of the same body, and sharers in the promise in Christ Jesus through the gospel" (Eph 3:6). The Gentiles do not constitute an alternative to Israel but are to be one with Israel.

How Shall We Build?

I could not help highlighting this issue, but it is clear that our main concern, in the context of *lectio divina*, is not so much of a theological nature as of a spiritual and ascetic one. Far from moving us into an attitude of self-complacency and false enthusiasm, the Letter to the Ephesians is a continual call to change and conversion, and this is true of the passage on which we are commenting.

What is required of one who desires to participate in the construction of the edifice, who wants to be a "living stone" of the Church? St. Paul in the First Letter to the Corinthians used the metaphor of Church-edifice in order to respond to this question. His discourse is of special interest inasmuch as it applies to those who are called to "preside" over the labor of constructing the house of God. These are the leaders, pastors and preachers (in 1 Corinthians 3, Paul, Cephas and even Apollo are specifically mentioned). Let us listen to Paul's words:

> For we are God's servants, working together; you are God's field, God's building. According to the grace of God given to me, like a skilled master builder I laid a foundation, and someone else is building on it. Each builder must choose with care how to build on it. For no one can lay any foundation other than the one that has been laid; that foundation is Jesus Christ. Now if anyone builds on the foundation with gold, silver, precious stones, wood, hay, straw—the work of each builder will become visible, for the Day will disclose it, because it will be revealed with fire, and the fire will test what sort of work each has done.
>
> —1 CORINTHIANS 3:9-13

Even today, building fraud is a problem in some places. More sand than cement is added to the mixture, and after a few years the building begins to crumble.

That which determines the goodness of our works is not so much what we do as the intention with which we do it. As the soul is to the body or the root is to the tree, so, too, is intention to our actions. Any good builder knows how to use a plumb line to determine whether or not a wall is truly straight and to discover any protrusions or buckling. Scripture offers us several "plumb lines" or rules with which we can measure and rectify our intentions.

One of these is that which the apostle recommends to the Colossians: "Whatever your task, put yourselves into it, as done for the Lord and not for your masters" (Col 3:23). Another is his advice to the Corinthians: "So, whether you eat or drink, or whatever you do, do everything for the glory of God" (1 Cor 10:31). And in the Letter to the Galatians he says: "Am I now seeking human approval, or God's approval?" (Galatians 1:10).

We need to imitate hunters who are taking aim. In order to concentrate their vision, they close the left eye. We need to close the eye that looks to humanity and keep wide open the one that looks to God.

For Whose Glory?

Already in the second century, along the lines of the Letter to the Ephesians, the Shepherd of Hermas speaks of the Church as a very tall tower built on water with more or less polished stones.[9] This calls to mind the theme of the Church as anti-Babel, a theme also found in the Acts description of Pentecost (see Acts 2:5-13).

At one time it was thought that the sin of the tower of Babel's builders was that they were trying to challenge God. Today, however, we believe that the builders were pious and religious people who wanted to build a temple of superimposed terraces. Ruins of such buildings, called ziggurats, can still be found in Mesopotamia.

So where is their sin? It is in the intention with which they built the tower. They said to one another: "Come, let us build ourselves a city, and a tower with its top in the heavens, and let us make a name for ourselves; otherwise we shall be scattered abroad upon the face of the whole earth" (Genesis 11:4). They desired to build a temple to the godhead not for the glory of God but rather to make a name for themselves.

On the Day of Pentecost the apostles began to construct a tower whose top touches heaven, the Church. They did not, however, do so to make a name for themselves but to make a name for God. It is written that everyone understood them because they were "speaking about God's deeds of power" (Acts 2:11). They were no longer interested in establishing who among them was the greatest. They had stopped focusing on themselves and were now concentrated on Christ.

God does not ask the impossible of us. He does not ask us never to feel the desire to affirm ourselves and to succeed in life, or never to be touched by the temptation of career. These things are inherent in our nature. What counts are the choices I freely make throughout my life.

It is like navigating against the wind: The helm cannot be left alone for even an instant; otherwise the boat will begin to go in a direction other than the one desired. Lent is not just a time of self-deprivation; it is also a time for correcting one's path, for rectifying one's intentions. This, perhaps, is the best spiritual exercise we can do during Lent.

A small public confession on my part is not out of line at this point. This address on the rectitude of intentions did not want to come together. Everything was on hold until a small voice within asked me the most obvious of questions: "And you? What is your intention in preaching about the purity of intentions?" The Gospel text at Mass that day seemed to have been written to help me (and not just me) make an examination of conscience:

The scribes and the Pharisees sit on Moses' seat; therefore, do whatever they teach you and follow it; but do not do as they do, for they do not practice what they teach. They tie up heavy burdens, hard to bear, and lay them on the shoulders of others; but they themselves are unwilling to lift a finger to move them. They do all their deeds to be seen by others.

—MATTHEW 23:2-5

This text was enough to point out my sin and to bring forth a good confession. Then this reflection, good or bad as it might be, immediately came together in my mind, and I was able to write it down.

The Letter to the Ephesians offers us a brief but theologically dense formula to help us orient or rectify our intentions: "To him be glory in the church and in Christ Jesus to all generations, forever and ever. Amen" (Eph 3:21).

CHAPTER TWO

There Is One Body, One Spirit

*T*oday we encounter the inability to change human logic and to bring about peace in the world. This frustration makes us feel more urgently the need to bring to fruition God's plan for the Church. As is stated in one of the Eucharistic prayers, "Your people may stand forth in a world torn by strife and discord as a sign of oneness and peace."[1]

The Letter to the Ephesians discusses the subject of how to maintain peace and increase unity among the community of believers:

> I, therefore, the prisoner of the Lord, beg you to lead a life worthy of the calling to which you have been called, with all humility and gentleness, with patience, bearing with one another in love, making every effort to maintain the unity of the Spirit in the bond of peace. There is one body and one Spirit, just as you were called to the one hope of your calling, one Lord, one faith, one baptism, one God and Father of all, who is above all and through all and in all.
>
> —EPHESIANS 4:1-6

Unity and Diversity in the Church

Around the year A.D. 90 Pope Clement wrote the famous "Letter to the Church of Corinth" in order to encourage it to reestablish its internal unity and peace. There the Pope simply paraphrased ideas from the Letter to the Ephesians:

> Why is it that you harbor strife, bad temper, dissension, schism, and quarreling? Do we not have one God, one Christ, one Spirit of grace which was poured out on us? And

is there not one calling in Christ? Why do we rend and tear asunder Christ's members and raise a revolt against our own body?[2]

The words "one body, one Spirit, one hope…one God who is Father" do not delineate the parameters for maintaining unity; rather they are the foundations of Christian unity.[3] We must be united not so that we may be able to be one body and to have one God as Father but because we are one body and have one God who is Father.

At this point there is an abrupt linguistic change in the text. Words that indicate unity (*only, one*) are replaced by words that indicate particularity: *some, others, each one*:

> Each of us was given grace according to the measure of Christ's gift…. The gifts he gave were that some would be apostles, some prophets, some evangelists, some pastors and teachers.
>
> —EPHESIANS 4:7, 11

We can find no greater clarity on these two essential components of the Church, unity and diversity. It is not a matter of finding balance between two opposing needs. Diversity is not a limit or a corrective to unity but, rather, the only way of manifesting it, because it deals with the unity of persons and not of things. Diversity is for collaboration. It exists

> to equip the saints for the work of ministry, for building up the body of Christ, until all of us come to the unity of the

faith and of the knowledge of the Son of God, to maturity, to the measure of the full stature of Christ.

—EPHESIANS 4:12-13

On this point the language of Ephesians is very close to that of 1 Corinthians 12:6-7: "And there are varieties of activities, but it is the same God who activates all of them in everyone. To each is given the manifestation of the Spirit for the common good."

If by the word "sacrament" we intend what is common to all, and by "charism" what is particular to each one, we can say that the sacraments are the gifts given to the community for the good of the individuals, while charisms are gifts given to individuals for the good of the entire community. Sacraments are given to the Church in order to sanctify each person, charisms are gifts given to each person in order to sanctify the Church. The final goal is the same for everyone: to promote communion, to create *koinonia*.

Church Communion

This communion is what I would like to reflect on here, calling to mind the urgent invitation of *Novo millennio ineunte*:

This is the other important area in which there has to be commitment and planning on the part of the universal Church and the particular Churches: the domain of communion (*koinonia*), which embodies and reveals the very essence of the mystery of the Church…. It is in building this communion of love that the Church appears as

25

> "sacrament," as the "sign and instrument of intimate union with God and of the unity of the human race" (*Lumen gentium*, n. 1).[4]

These words constitute the final landing place of ecclesiological renewal, initiated almost two centuries ago by Möhler with the work *Unity in the Church*. Carried on by Cardinal Newman, this renewal found fruition in the ecclesiology of the Second Vatican Council, according to which the Church is essentially a communion rooted in love.

Two concepts can help us to understand the novelty of this ecclesiology with regard to the previous one: the concepts of state and nation. *Nation* indicates people, social reality and individuals; *state* indicates the organization of this reality: the government that maintains it, the constitution by which it is governed, the various authorities (judicial, legislative and executive) and the symbols that represent it. It is not the nation that is at the service of the state but the state that is at the service of the nation.

We might say, by analogy, that at one time the Church was seen, above all, as the state, while now it is seen above all as a nation, as the people of God. At one time it was seen primarily as a hierarchy; now it is seen primarily as a *koinonia*. Clearly both are essential. What would a state be without a nation? And what would a nation be without a state, if not an amorphous multitude of people in perennial conflict with one another? What has changed, however, are not the constitutive elements of the Church but rather the priority among them. *Novo millennio ineunte* concludes:

While the wisdom of the law, by providing precise rules for participation, attests to the hierarchical structure of the Church and averts any temptation to arbitrariness or unjustified claims, the spirituality of communion, by prompting a trust and openness wholly in accord with the dignity and responsibility of every member of the People of God, supplies institutional reality with a soul.[5]

The Spirit: "Soul of the Church"

Let's return to the text of Ephesians. All of the reasons for unity listed here are summarized in the expression: "One body, one Spirit." The word *body*, applied to the Church in the letters of the so-called "captivity," is no longer a simple metaphor indicating the interdependence and necessary collaboration of the various members, but indicates the reality of the Church inasmuch as it is the body of Christ, organically united to the head.

This profound sense of "one body" is truly revealed by the expression that accompanies it, "one Spirit." The body of Christ has a vital principle that unites its various members with the head, and this principle is none other than the Holy Spirit, who is communicated by the head to its body. From this we get the famous image, dear to Augustine, of the Holy Spirit as "soul of the Church":

What the soul is to the human body, the Holy Spirit is to the body of Christ, which is the Church. The Holy Spirit does in the whole Church what the soul does in all the parts of one body.[6]

The image of the "soul of the Church" helps us to understand something important: The Holy Spirit does not effect the unity of the Church from the outside; it doesn't just push for unity, nor does it limit itself to requiring that the Church be united. It "is" and it "fosters" unity. It is not only the efficient cause but also the material cause; it is that by which the Church is united. The phrase, so dear to the liturgy, "In the unity of the Holy Spirit," signifies "in the unity which is the same Holy Spirit."

One could object, but if this is true, isn't unity already assured by the presence of the one Holy Spirit? Why should we worry so much about this? I offer the following response: The Holy Spirit is love and fosters unity through love, infusing charity. Unity is not imposed but offered; it is both realized and yet still to be fulfilled, because it is the fruit of grace and freedom. This is why Jesus prays that his disciples "be one" (Jn 17:11). As living stones, believers must participate actively in the construction of unity.

Back to Pentecost

The best way to understand the nature of the unity of the Church is to return to the Pentecost event. There the Church is revealed as a sign of unity among all people. But how is such unity created? "All of them," it is written, "were filled with the Holy Spirit" (Acts 2:4). The Holy Spirit is the uncreated love of the Father for the Son and of the Son for the Father. Therefore, saying that everyone was full of the Holy Spirit is like saying that they were full of the love of God, that the apostles had an overwhelming experience of the love of God.

It was as if the floodgates of the sky opened, and the ocean of love, which is the Trinity, poured out its waters over the earth. The apostles were baptized—that is, submerged in the love of God. Now God the Father could realize the goal for which he had created the world.

Paul clearly confirms this: "God's love has been poured into our hearts through the Holy Spirit that has been given to us" (Rom 5:5). This is a description of what happened at Pentecost and what happens for every believer at baptism. It corresponds to what Acts narrates: "All of them were filled with the Holy Spirit" (Acts 2:4).

This love of God, as St. Thomas Aquinas explains, is at once the love with which God loves us (*amor quo Deus nos diligit*) and the love by which God makes it possible for us to love him (*amor quo ipse nos dilectores sui facit*).[7] It is a new capacity for loving God and neighbor, which we call infused love or the theological virtue of charity. At the moment, therefore, in which the apostles were filled with God's love for them, they were also filled with love for one another.

I cannot imagine Pentecost in the way that it has been traditionally pictured by artists: everyone motionless and composed, their arms placed devoutly across their chests, their faces devoid of expression. I prefer the images created among the young Christian communities of Africa out of their own experience of Pentecost. I have in mind a particular image from Cameroon, part of a series called *Jesus Mafa*. The apostles are looking at each other and smiling ecstatically. Some are reaching out toward heaven, while others are hiding their faces in their hands because of the excessive light. Only Mary is seated peacefully, calm and composed. The reason is clear: She has already had her Pentecost, so what is happening does not take her by surprise. She sang about the "sober drunkenness" of the Spirit in the *Magnificat*.

Thus, ecclesial *koinonia* is born from the experience of being loved by God, who creates the need for and the possibility of loving one another. This is visible in what follows Pentecost: The believers were "of one heart and soul" (Acts 4:32). Collegiality as a lived reality is also born here. Before Pentecost Peter usually spoke in the first person singular; for example, "Even though I must die with you, I will not deny you!" (Mt 26:35). Now he uses plural pronouns: "All of us are witnesses" (Acts 2:32). A new subject appears, that of collegiality: Peter "standing with the eleven" (Acts 2:14).

Two Paths toward Unity

Pentecost is the founding event of the Church, and one must always refer to it in order to know what the Church is and what it must be. Pentecost contains the "DNA" of the Church. But to separate the story of Pentecost from the rest of the Acts of the Apostles is to fall into grave error. The Spirit works for unity of the elect in two different but complementary ways, one extraordinary and one ordinary. The first we describe as *ex opere operato*, by which the Holy Spirit creates unity alone, and the other as *ex opere operantis*, by which we create unity along with the Holy Spirit.

Extraordinary or charismatic unity is what the Holy Spirit accomplished on the Day of Pentecost, among "devout Jews from every nation" (Acts 2:5). Such is also the unity among Jews and Gentiles that was realized for the first time in the home of Cornelius the centurion (see Acts 10-11). At this stage of the Church's life there is a prevalence of divine initiative that manifests itself in unpredictable, powerful, creative ways. There is neither time nor need for discussions, deliberations or decrees. The apostles themselves are being carried. The Holy Spirit leads, and the institution can do nothing but follow.

The unity that results from this action is charismatic in nature: comprised of praise, enthusiasm, joy, stupor and proclamations of the Lord Jesus. It is not merely a doctrinal unity or a unity of faith, but rather it is complete: The believers are "of one heart and soul" (Acts 4:32). This unity is a kind of "fusion by fire."

But this unity alone does not last long. A second movement of the Spirit is necessary in order to help the apostles overcome the tensions of living together. Soon after Pentecost there arises the question of the distribution of provisions among the widows (see Acts 6:1-6). How will the young community maintain unity? The apostles gather together and create the role of deacon. Authority intervenes when charismatic spontaneity is no longer enough.

A stronger tension arrives after the conversion of the pagans. The unity newly created between Jews and Gentiles is threatened by schism, as certain Judaizers claim that the Gentiles should also practice circumcision and observe the Law of Moses. And this time, how does the Spirit move? "The apostles and the elders met together to consider this matter. After there had been much debate," the agreement reached was announced to the Church with the words: "It has seemed good to the Holy Spirit and to us" (see Acts 15:1-31).

Thus, in matters of discipline rather than faith, the Holy Spirit also works through patient confrontation, mutual listening and compromise. He works through human structures and ministers selected by Jesus. What impresses me most in the story in which Paul resists Peter (see Galatians 2:14) is not so much Paul's frankness as Peter's humility. Peter accepts Paul's argument and appears to take into account the position that he himself supported at the Council of Jerusalem.

Embolisms in the Body

The exhortation we read at the beginning of the fourth chapter of the letter concerns this ordinary path to unity:

> I therefore, the prisoner in the Lord, beg you to lead a life worthy of the calling to which you have been called, with all humility and gentleness, with patience, bearing with one another in love, making every effort to maintain the unity of the Spirit in the bond of peace.
>
> —EPHESIANS 4:1-3

The author returns to this point at the end of the chapter, demonstrating the depth of his concern for unity:

> Put away from you all bitterness and wrath and anger and wrangling and slander, together with all malice, and be kind to one another, tenderhearted, forgiving one another, as God in Christ has forgiven you.
>
> —EPHESIANS 4:31-32

Embolisms pose a mortal danger to the human body. Abnormal particles called emboli obstruct veins and arteries and, if not cleared in time, hinder the free circulation of blood. This can cause great damage, leading to paralysis or even death. The Church, which is the body of Christ, faces its own kind of embolisms. These obstacles to communion include the refusal to forgive, lasting hostility and the bitterness, wrath, anger, slander and malice cited above.

If we want to "maintain unity of the spirit in the bond of peace," it is necessary to periodically take an x-ray—that is, a thorough examination of conscience—to be sure that there are no blockages for which we are responsible. At the level of ecumenism, we must work patiently to remove the enormous barriers that have been built between the churches. This work has to take place at the capillary level: between communities and denominations; within each church—for example, between clergy and laypeople—and finally between individuals.

Unity Multiplies Charisms

St. Augustine never grew tired of offering the examples of the miracles that occur whenever one cultivates this love through unity. He wrote that when people hear the Apostle Paul list all of the great gifts given by the Holy Spirit to the Church, it can make them sad because they feel that they do not have a share in those gifts. He suggests that they should love unity because everything that is in one church member is also in them. In putting away envy, whatever one has belongs to everyone and whatever others have belongs to each one.[8]

In the Church community the charism of one becomes the charism of everyone. Only the eye of the body has the ability to see. But is it possible that the eye functions alone? Doesn't the whole body benefit from its ability to see? If a stone were to hit one's eye, would the hand remain calm and motionless, since the violence is not directed toward it? The same occurs in the body of Christ: what every member is and does, it is and does for everyone. The indication that one possesses the Spirit is not the ability to speak in tongues or to do miracles, but a love of unity. St. Augustine said, "You know that you have the Holy Spirit when you allow the heart to adhere to unity through sincere charity."[9]

Pope Clement's *Letter to the Corinthians*, which I mentioned at the beginning, ends with a solemn prayer for harmony and peace—not only among the citizens and leaders of Corinth and among the leaders of the Church—but also among all peoples and creatures of the earth. Let us conclude today's reflection with this prayer:

> You humble the pride of the arrogant,
> overrule the plans of the nations,
> raise up the humble and humble the haughty."[10]...
> Give us and all who live on the earth harmony and
>   peace....
> And grant that we may be obedient to your
>   almighty and glorious name,
> and to our rulers and governors on earth....
> Grant them, Lord, health, peace, harmony, and
>   stability,
> so that they may give no offense in administering
> the government you have given them.
> For it is you, Master, the heavenly "king of eternity,"
> who give the sons of men glory and honor and
>   authority
> over the earth's people....
> We praise you...

through the high priest and guardian of our souls,
   Jesus Christ.
Through him be the glory and the majesty to you
   now and for all generations and forevermore.
Amen.[11]

CHAPTER THREE

Christ Loved the Church

*C*hrist loved the church and gave himself up for her, in order to make her holy by cleansing her with the washing of water by the word, so as to present the church to himself in splendor, without a spot or wrinkle or anything of the kind—yes, so that she may be holy and without blemish. In the same way, husbands should love their wives as they do their own bodies. He who loves his wife loves himself. For no one ever hates his own body, but he nourishes and tenderly cares for it, just as Christ does for the church, because we are members of his body. "For this reason a man will leave his father and mother and be joined to his wife, and the two will become one flesh." This is a great mystery, and I am applying it to Christ and the church.

—EPHESIANS 5:25-32

The images used in the Letter to the Ephesians to illustrate the mystery of the Church—edifice, body, spouse—flow into one another. The original image of an edifice is preserved in Ephesians 4:12, which speaks of "building up the body of Christ." The image of body is preserved in that of spouse, in that the two become "one flesh."

However, there is something new here. While the image of body expresses the unity between Christ and the Church, the image of spouse highlights the irreducible otherness of each. The union between Christ and the Church is an interpersonal one, between beings who are face-to-face as an "I" and a "you." The union of Christ and the Church reflects the unity of humanity and divinity in Christ: It is a union without confusion.

The theme of God as bridegroom of his people permeates the Old Testament and is the foundation of the concept of covenant. Jesus presented himself as the fulfillment of that nuptial promise, as the one who realizes "the new and eternal covenant" between God and humanity. He implicitly attributes to himself the title of bridegroom in the parable of the wedding feast (see Mt 22:1-14) and also in the parable of the ten bridesmaids (see Mt 25:1-13). He also adopts this title when he claims, "The wedding guests cannot fast while the bridegroom is with them, can they?" (Mk 2:19).

The Church as Bride

But in its earthly phase, is the Church truly a bride or simply Christ's fiancée? The Church is both at the same time. What the First Letter of John says about divine sonship can be applied. The Church is already a bride, but that which it will become has not yet been revealed (see 1 Jn 3:2). The bride in her full status, who can no longer be separated from the spouse is the one Revelation 19:7-9 prophetically presents at the wedding feast in the heavenly Jerusalem.

The Letter to the Ephesians has given more significance to the spousal theme than any other text in the New Testament, drawing from it important practical consequences for the life of the community and the Christian view of marriage. People of old knew a literary genre called *epithalamy* or "nuptial song." An example is Psalm 45, which begins, "My heart overflows with a goodly theme; I address my verses to the king." It was written for the wedding of "the most handsome of men" to the queen who stands "at his right hand in the gold of Ophir." This psalm has been applied to the liturgy of the wedding between Christ and the Church.

The Letter to the Ephesians is also a type of epithalamy. The author evokes a nuptial ritual, used in antiquity, in which the day before her marriage the bride would take a bath in sacred water. This nuptial bath was considered part of the rites that initiate the wedding.[1] The nuptial bath of the Church is the blood of Christ. He "freed us from our sins by his blood" (Rv 1:5). The bath is prolonged through baptism, "the washing of water by the word" (Eph 5:26). An Easter homily of the second century reads:

> Wanting to destroy the work of the woman and to rescue her, who, in the beginning, came forth from the rib of Adam, the bearer of death, he opens his own sacred ribs from which pour out blood and water, initiation to the spiritual and mystical nuptials, sign of adoption and regeneration.[2]

Patristic writers make this symbolism even more explicit:

> It is from His side...that Christ formed His church, just as He formed Eve from the side of Adam.... Just as then He took the rib from Adam when he was in a deep sleep, so now He gave us blood and water after His death, first the water and then the blood. But what was then a deep slumber is now a death, so that you may know that this death is henceforth sleep. Have you seen how Christ unites to Himself His bride?[3]

The wedding of Christ and the Church is not modeled on that of man and woman, but rather the opposite is true. "This is a great mystery, and I am applying it to Christ and the church."

Psychologists have cast heavy suspicion on the spiritual marriage of the mystics. The descriptions of their experiences, these psychologists say, closely resemble amorous experiences. What the mystics say of divine love very closely resembles what happens in human love! Is not the mystical marriage with God nothing more than a "mystification" of natural marriage, its sublimation or perhaps its surrogate? Very few are able to explain Bernini's *St. Teresa in Ecstasy*, in the church of Santa Maria della Vittoria in Rome, without falling into this common trap.

To this one must respond: Why not consider the opposite hypothesis—that is, that natural marriage is imitation while mystical marriage is reality? Is it not better to consider sexual union to be a symbol, a parable and a striving for that other "completion" of which the mystics have had a foretaste? Doesn't union in the flesh carry in itself signs of imperfection, uncertainty and the yearning for something longer, lasting and different?

It is significant that it took a person like Goethe to recognize this. He concludes the amorous affair between Faust and Margaret with the words: "All things ephemeral are symbols only, the inaccessible here [in heaven] is known finally."[4] Perfect union, unattainable in human marriage, becomes reality only in heaven, in the full and eternal union of spirits.

Nor is it fair to consider the symbolism of Christ as bridegroom and Church as bride a sign of male chauvinism that privileges the role of men over women. It is true that in such symbolism the role of head belongs to the bridegroom and the subordinate role goes to the bride, but it is also true that the Church here represents both men and women without distinction. Traditionally the title "bride of Christ" has been reserved to consecrated women, especially cloistered ones, because the symbolic correlation is more evident in them. They are like an epiphany of the Church as bride. However, the soul of every believer, female or male, is theologically the bride of Christ.

One Body

Christ and the Church, according to the Letter to the Ephesians, are one flesh. Where does this "great mystery" become present, and what is its sacramental sign? To be even more explicit, where does the "consummation" of this marriage take place? The answer can be found in the words, "Take, eat, this is my body": the Eucharist.

According to the apostle, the immediate effect of marriage is that the husband's body becomes the wife's and vice versa (see 1 Cor 7:4). This is what occurs spiritually in the Eucharist. The incorruptible and life-giving flesh of the Incarnate Word becomes "my" flesh. The effect of the Eucharist, St. Cyril states, is that it makes us flesh and blood relatives of Christ.[5]

So, too, the reverse is true: My flesh and my humanity become Christ's; they are truly his. This can have a great impact on how one lives eucharistic communion. In his earthly life Christ knew the male existence and not the female one. He apparently did not know illness and certainly did not come to know old age. He did not know what it meant to be married and have children or to be a person of color. Yet all of this that was "lacking" in the Incarnation of Christ is now fulfilled in the Eucharist.

He comes to abide in me, just as I am. I can review all the small details of my life: my past, my most secret desires, my weaknesses, everything. He has not lived all of this in his own flesh, but in the Eucharist he lives all of these details of my existence. In a certain sense he lives in women what it is to be woman, in the infirm what it is to be infirm, in the depressed their depression, in parents the experience of having children, in the aged what it is to be old. We are for him, as Blessed Elizabeth of the Trinity used to say, a kind of "additional humanity."[6] What a grace it is to receive Communion with this certainty of faith!

The analogy between human marriage and the union of Christ and the Church lies in the fact that both are based on love: "Christ loved the Church." But what exactly did he love, we ask ourselves, since at the moment in which he gave up his life, the Church did not yet exist? The exegetes explain that he loved "the Church preexistent in God in virtue of his pre-temporal election and determination."[7] Christ loved the Church with the same love with which God loved humanity in creating it. Let us listen to how Catherine of Siena describes the love of something that does not yet exist:

> Eternal Father, how did you come to create this creature of yours?... [Your own] fire, then, compelled you. O ineffable love, though in your light you saw all the iniquities your creature was to commit against your infinite goodness, you pretended not to see, and set your eyes on the beauty of your creature with whom you fell in love like a fool or one drunk with love, and in love you gave it being in your image and likeness. [8]

Gabriel Marcel says that according to Christian Metaphysics, "to be is to be loved." The creature exists because it has been loved. This is especially true of the Church. She exists inasmuch as she is loved.

To Love as Christ Loves

One can derive an important consequence from the words of St. Catherine: Christ has loved the Church, despite the iniquities that she was to commit, so who are we to find in the Church's weaknesses and misery a reason not to love her but to judge her instead? We who are filled with sin?

Do we actually think that Jesus doesn't know the sins of the Church as well as we do? Did he not know for whom he was dying? Did he not know that one of his disciples had betrayed him and that another was denying him and that the rest were fleeing? He, however, loved this real Church, not an imaginary and ideal one. He died to make her "holy and without blemish" (Eph 5:27), not because she was holy and without blemish. He loves the Church "in hope," not just for what she is but also for what she is called to be and will be: the heavenly Jerusalem "prepared as a bride adorned for her husband" (Rv 21:2).

Christ loved the Church and gave himself for her so that she would be "without stain." And the Church would be without stain if we were not a part of it! The Church would have one less wrinkle if I committed one less sin. Martin Luther criticized Erasmus of Rotterdam for remaining in the Catholic Church despite its corruption, but Erasmus answered him: "I put up with this Church, in the hope that one day it will become better, just as it is constrained to put up with me in the hope that one day I will become better."[9]

We should ask Christ to forgive all of our inconsiderate judgments and the many offenses we heap upon his bride, and as a result upon him as well. Try to tell a man who is truly in love that his bride is ugly or a "good-for-nothing," and see if you can take his ire. Speaking of his homeland during one of the darkest periods of the last war, Saint-Exupéry wrote:

> Since I am one with the people of France, I shall never reject my people, whatever they may do. I shall never preach against them in the hearing of others. Whenever it is possible to take their defence, I shall defend them. If they cover me with shame I shall lock up that shame in my heart and be silent. Whatever at such a time I shall think of them, I shall never bear witness against them. Does a husband go from house to house crying out to his neighbours that his wife is a strumpet? Is it thus that he can preserve his honour? No, for his wife is one with his home. No, for he cannot establish his dignity against her. Let him go home to her, and there unburden himself of his anger.[10]

Once you have "reentered the house," once you have wept with the Church, once you have humbled yourself at its feet, God can command you as he has done in the past to raise your voice against "the wounds of the Church." But not before. The saints have applied to the Church that which Job said about God, according to the Vulgate version of the Bible then in use: "Even if God were to kill me, I would still have recourse to him" (see Jb 13:15).[11]

Friends of the Bridegroom

The affirmation of the Letter to the Ephesians, "Christ loved the Church," contains an implicit question, "Do you?" The sign of Christ's love for the Church is that he "gave himself up for her." So, too, the sign that we love the Church will be that we give ourselves to her. "Ourselves" means our time, energy, prayers, sacrifice, affection— sacrificing our personal ambitions, projects and interests. The biblical image that expresses what we should be for the Church is friends of the bridegroom! John the Baptist explains:

> He who has the bride is the bridegroom. The friend of the bridegroom, who stands and hears him, rejoices greatly at the bridegroom's voice. For this reason my joy has been fulfilled. He must increase, but I must decrease.
>
> —JOHN 3:29-30

"He must increase, but I must decrease": We must be the friends of the bridegroom, not his rivals in love. We should not be substitutes for the groom, but rather we should serve him. One of Pascal's thoughts can help us understand what this is about:

> It is unjust that men should attach themselves to me, even though they do it with pleasure and voluntarily. I should deceive those in whom I had created this desire for I am not the end of any, and I have not the wherewithal to satisfy them. Am I not about to die? And thus the object of their attachment will die.... I ought to warn those who are ready to consent to a lie that they ought not to believe it, whatever advantage comes to me from it; and likewise that they

ought not to attach themselves to me; for they ought to spend their life and their care in pleasing God, or in seeking Him.[12]

The virtue proper to the friend of the bridegroom is jealousy. The apostle Paul, another great friend of the bridegroom, writes: "I feel a divine jealousy for you, for I promised you in marriage to one husband, to present you as a chaste virgin to Christ" (2 Cor 11:2). Zeal comes from jealousy (zeal and jealousy are both translations of the Greek word zelos!). This was characteristic of Elijah: "I have been very zealous for the Lord, the God of hosts" (1 Kings 19:10). It was also characteristic of Jesus: "Zeal for your house will consume me" (Jn 2:17), and it has always been characteristic of the great servants of the Church.

Zeal is not often talked about anymore; the word has taken on negative connotations. But it is what the gospel needs: zealous bishops, zealous priests, zealous conse-crated men and women. The Letter to the Ephesians includes in the armor of God "as shoes for your feet the zeal of proclaiming the gospel of peace" (Eph 6:15).[13]

Service to the See of Peter

During the Great Jubilee of 2000 a Roman congregation organized a spiritual ritual for its members using the theme "The Spirituality of Service to the See of Peter." The Pope is the representative on earth of the Church's bridegroom; he is the first among the "friends of the bridegroom." The direct work under him in the Roman curia cannot be reduced to bureaucratic labor. Such work should have soul, the soul with which "Christ loved the church and gave himself up for her."

Working in the curia needs to be a way of realizing the universal call to holiness. A good program in this regard is the one that Peter outlines for the "elders." He encourages them to "tend the flock of God that is in your charge, exercising the oversight, not under compulsion but willingly, as God would have you do it—not for sordid gain but eagerly. Do not lord it over those in your charge, but be examples to the flock" (1 Pt 5:2-3).

The Roman See, according to the martyr St. Ignatius, is called to "preside over the agape"[14]—that is, preside for charity and in charity. A climate of openness, of trust, of collaboration between the center and the rest of the Church, depends greatly on how much people feel welcomed by the associates of the Holy Father. It is not always possible to keep everyone happy, but even when one cannot go along with what is requested, the debt of love remains (see Rom 13:8). This is expressed in courtesy, gentility, graciousness, and patience.

St. Bernard, in his *De consideratione*, outlines for Pope Eugene III the qualities of a good member of the curia. His is a very demanding profile, but it is worth keeping in mind, at least as an ideal:

> Take in not those who wish office or who run after it, but those who hesitate and those who decline it; even force them and compel them to enter. I think your spirit will find rest among such men who are not impudent, but modest and respectful; besides God alone they fear nothing, they hope for nothing except from God. They look not to the hands of those who approach [seeking to serve the Church],

but to their needs. And they manfully stand up for the afflicted and judge fairly for the meek of the earth. They are men of suitable character, proven sanctity, ready obedience, and quiet patience. They are subject to discipline, severe in censuring, catholic in faith, faithful in service; inclined toward peace, and desirous of unity. These are men who are upright in judgment, farsighted in counsel, prudent in commands, industrious in organization, energetic in actions, modest in speech.... They are not anxious in the care of their own property nor eager for that of another; they are not prodigal with their own possessions but are everywhere and in all things circumspect.... They are careful about their own reputations but do not envy another's. They habitually devote themselves to prayer, and in every undertaking place more confidence in it than in their own industry or labor.[15]

St. Catherine of Siena: Model of Prayer

Service to the See of Peter is best expressed in praying for the Pope. "While Peter was kept in prison, the church prayed fervently to God for him" (Acts 12:5), and it was the Church's prayer that caused the chains to fall from his hands. St. Paul, a zealous Christian leader though not a pope, frequently asked his followers and coworkers to pray for him. He kept them updated as to his "toil and hardship,...[and] anxiety for all the churches. Who is weak, and I am not weak? Who is made to stumble, and I am not indignant?" (2 Cor 11:27-29).

It is not difficult to intuit how all of this repeats itself for the one who carries on his back "anxiety for all the churches." We can imagine how scandals that afflict the Church would cause his heart to tremble. We can take an intimate part in these sufferings by lifting them up in prayer as much as possible. On crossing the Tiber, by Castel Sant'Angelo, in front of via Conciliazione, one can admire a statue of St. Catherine of Siena, placed there in 1962 at the end of the fifth centenary celebration of her canonization. The saint is in an unusual pose: curved forward like an exhausted vagrant, holding herself up on a staff. It is a reminder that Catherine, during the final Lent of her life, walked daily to St. Peter's to pray that the Roman populace would reconcile with Pope Urban VI. She wrote to her confessor, Blessed Raymond of Capua:

> And at the hours of Terce I rise up from Mass, and if you looked you would see a dead woman walking to St. Peter's, where I work again in the little bark of the holy Church. There I stay until near Vespers, and I would love never to leave that place whether by day or night until I see this people steadied and strengthened a little with their father.[16]

The dogma of the communion of saints is beautiful. It permits us to believe that Catherine continues to pray not just that the Roman people but that the whole Christian people might be united with the Holy Father. The saints continue to exercise in heaven the charisms that they exercised on earth.

If I were asked again to speak at a retreat on the spirituality of service to the See of Peter, I would have St. Catherine speak in my place. I would suggest, read the letters of St. Catherine. She radiates to the highest degree the virtues needed for service to the See of Peter: affection, humility, obedience in every test, but also incredible freedom, straightforwardness, *parrhesia*. Being a good Tuscan woman, she called the Pope her Babbo, "sweet daddy," yet she had no problem writing these words to him:

> You are father and lord of the universal body of the Christian religion; we are all under the wings of your Holiness: as to authority, you can do everything, but as to seeing, you can do no more than one man; so your sons must of necessity watch and care with clean hearts and without any servile fear over what may be for the honour of God and the safety and honour of you and the flocks that are beneath your crook. And I know that your Holiness is very desirous of having people to help you.[17]

One can say that many of the saints, following the example of Christ, have loved the Church and given themselves for her, but none more than Catherine. In the homily for being named Doctor of the Church, on October 4, 1970, Paul VI read emotionally the words written by her as she was dying:

> O eternal God, accept the sacrifice of my life on behalf of this mystical body of the holy Church. I have nothing else to give except what you have given me. Take my heart, then, and squeeze it out over the face of the bride.[18]

Regarding her daily walks to St. Peter's, she had written to her confessor: "My life is consumed and shed for this sweet Bride: I by this road, and the glorious martyrs with blood."[19] She saw her life as a type of martyrdom for the Church.

Let us join in St. Catherine's fiery prayer, which invites the lovers of the Church to form a buttressing wall of prayer:

O sweetest love, you found in yourself the need of the holy
Church, and the remedy that she needs, and you have given
it to her, that is, the prayer of your servants, which you seek
to make into a buttress that will support the wall of the holy
Church and in which the clemency of your Holy Spirit will
infuse fiery desires for its reformation.[20]

CHAPTER FOUR

"Son, Behold Your Mother!"

*C*hrist loved the church and gave himself up for her, in order to make her holy by cleansing her with the washing of water by the word, so as to present the church to himself in splendor, without a spot or wrinkle or anything of the kind—yes, so that she may be holy and without blemish.

—EPHESIANS 5:25-27

There has always been a tendency to identify this image of the Church "in splendor, holy and without blemish" with the heavenly Church, in its fulfillment. One of the great exegetes from antiquity, Theodore of Mopsuestia, bases his whole lecture on Ephesians on this thesis. He writes:

> It is clear that the "holy and immaculate ones," as Paul understands it, will be us in the future age, through the working of the Spirit: these gifts will appear as they are in reality, whereas now we are living with the promise of attaining them, mediated by faith.[1]

Such a radical distinction between the present and future Church—one founded on hope and the other on reality—does not correspond to the ideas in the Letter to the Ephesians and to the New Testament in general. The Church is already the body of Christ, "the fullness of him who fills all in all" (Eph 1:23): already made "one spirit" with him (Eph 4:4). Therefore, we do not only possess the gift of the Spirit in hope but in reality, if only as the first fruit.

The Church and Mary

The Church is already "holy and without blemish" in its earthly stage, at least in one of its members: the Mother of Christ, whom Eastern Christianity honors with the title "All holy" (Panhagia) and Western Christianity with the title "Immaculate." The Church is also "holy and without blemish," in different ways in those whom it recognizes as models of holiness.

Reiterating *Lumen gentium* on this point, the encyclical *Redemptoris mater* says:

> "In the Most Holy Virgin the Church has already reached that perfection whereby she exists without spot or wrinkle." Hence, as Christians raise their eyes with faith to Mary in the course of their earthly pilgrimage, they "strive to increase in holiness."[2]

There is an iconographical tradition, found throughout central Italy, that identifies the bridal Church of Christ in Ephesians 5 with Mary. The Virgin leans her head on Christ's shoulder, who tenderly embraces her shoulder, while their hands are joined in the foreground. The words from Song of Songs are applied to Christ and Mary: "O that his left hand were under my head, and that his right hand embraced me!" (Song of Songs 2:6).

All of this has a biblical foundation. Mary and the Church are both seen as the new Eve and the new "daughter of Zion," who personifies the community of the new alliance. The exegete has difficulty determining whether the woman "clothed with the sun, with the moon under her feet" from Revelation 12 alludes to Mary or to the Church. Commentary in the Jerusalem Bible says that the woman represents the holy people of messianic times and, therefore, the struggling Church. But perhaps John is also thinking of Mary, the new Eve, daughter of Zion, who gave birth to the Messiah (see Jn 19:27).

"Standing near the cross of Jesus [was] his mother" (Jn 19:25). This time it is Adam who offers Eve the fruit of the tree of life to eat. The fruit is perfect obedience to the will of God. When Mary heard her Son say from the cross, "Father, into your hands I commend my spirit" (Lk 23:46), she could not help but feel that this was an invitation to follow him on this path. She began to adore, from deep within, the inscrutable will of the Father.

> [Mary] was united with Him by compassion as He died on the Cross. In this singular way she cooperated by her obedience, faith, hope and burning charity in the work of the Saviour in giving back supernatural life to souls. Wherefore she is our mother in the order of grace.[3]

This is the meaning behind many expressions that relate Mary to the Church. She is "the mirror of the Church," "the primacy of the Church," "the budding church." St. Francis uses a meaningful title, "the Virgin made Church."[4]

Mother Church

Mary "personifies" the Church beautifully because both are mothers of Christ. Augustine explained:

> The Church is a virgin that gives birth. It resembles Mary because it gives birth to the Lord. Is it possible that Mary did not give birth as a virgin but remained a virgin nevertheless? In this way, the Church also gives birth and is a virgin. It is important also to recall that it gives birth to Christ because the baptized are members of Christ.... And

if it gives birth to members of Christ, this is very similar to Mary (*Mariae simillima*).[5]

Tradition follows Augustine's line of thought, even up to the synthesis of *Lumen gentium*:

Mary and the Church are one mother and many mothers. ... The one without sin gave birth to the Head; the other, in the remission of sins, gave birth to the body for the Head. Both are mothers of Christ but neither gives birth to the whole without the other. For this reason, in the divinely inspired Scriptures, whatever it says in a universal way about the Virgin Mother Church, it also means in a particular way about the Virgin Mother Mary.[6]

The comparison with Mary enables us to progress in contemplating the Church, in that it emphasizes the maternal face of the Church. The title of mother adds something important to the images of edifice, body and spouse with which the Letter to the Ephesians has thus far presented her. The image of construction sheds light on the gradual becoming of the Church in salvation history; that of body, on unity with Christ; that of spouse, on otherness; that of mother, on causality or mediation with regard to the members of the body of Christ.

The patristic writers called the baptistery the womb in which the Church brings its children into the light, while the Word of God is the pure milk with which they are fed:

O mystic marvel! The universal Father is one, and one the universal Word; and the Holy Spirit is one and the same everywhere, and one is the only virgin mother. I love to call her the Church...pure as a virgin, loving as a mother. And

> calling her children to her, she nurses them with holy milk, viz. with the Word for childhood.[7] (see 1 Pt 2:2)

The baptistery is not, however, a womb that a person leaves at birth. Rather it is a womb into which one enters and in which one "nests" from the moment of conception. Our life in this world is the life of an embryo; it is a life of gestation. We truly come into the light on the day when we pass through the darkness of faith into the beatific vision. For this reason the liturgy calls the day of death one's "birthday," *dies natalis.*

The vital relationship between the fetus and the mother at the biological level is the same as the relationship between the believer and the Church at the supernatural level. Through the mother the fetus receives oxygen, food, blood, everything he or she needs. As we will see, the Church's title of mother not only has devotional meaning but is profoundly theological as well.

In light of these developments from tradition, let's listen once again to the words of Jesus to John: "Son, behold your mother!" Here we see that this implies something else: "Son, behold your mother, the Church!"

Children of the Church

The question arises: What is the Church for me? Is it truly a mother? St. Cyprian made a noteworthy remark: "You cannot have God for your Father if you have not the Church for your mother."[8]

We believers frequently complain, and justifiably, that the world and its mass media do not look beyond the surface of the Church in an effort to grasp its mystery of grace. They don't see beyond its political and social realities to its spiritual reality. They indulge in gossip about the Church rather than seek to understand its essence.

But is it only the world that falls into this error? Or do we, children of the Church, who are in close contact with the world and its human structures, do the same? Someone once said that "no one is great in the eyes of his own servants." We are the servants of the Church, those who see it from "inside the house," in its most human and least glorious aspects.

To test yourself in this regard, it is enough to ask, "What is the first thing that comes to mind when I hear the word *Church*?" Is it what the Letter to the Ephesians tells us? Or is it primarily the people, the tasks, the problems, the injustices you've suffered? Unfortunately we know what the world means when it says the word *Church*. It means "the Vatican" or "the hierarchy: the pope, bishops and priests." We risk adopting this misunderstanding ourselves, if we are not actually the cause of it.

The patristic writers applied Psalm 45 (the royal nuptial song!) jointly to Mary and the Church. This psalm, in its well-known version, says, "The king's daughter is all glorious within" (*omnis gloria filiae Regis ab intus*).[9] The beauty of the Church, like that of Mary, is the grace of which it is "full." Grace is in the Church as a pearl is in an oyster. The difference is that while the oyster produces the pearl, it is grace that generates the Church.

The Church can be compared to a stained glass window in a Gothic cathedral. I noticed this the first time I visited Chartres. Seen from the outside, the public way, the window is just a collection of dark pieces of glass held together by equally dark pieces of lead. But if you enter the cathedral and look at the same glass against the light, what a display of colors, figures and meaning! We have to place ourselves inside the Church in order to understand its mystery: inside not just institutionally but also with our hearts.

Love the Church

In the Lateran Museum there are two fragments of the famous inscription by Abercius, defined by archeologists as the "queen of Christian inscriptions." A Christian of Herapolis, in Asia Minor, at the end of the second century, Abercius had his epitaph inscribed in stone as he was dying. Using the the cryptic language of the "Discipline of the secret" (*Disciplina arcani*), used by Christians during the persecutions, he told the story of what he saw during his journeys throughout the world. It's worth getting acquainted with the epitaph because it can help us to recognize the eyes through which one can see the Church today:

> Abercius by name. I am the disciple of a
> venerable shepherd....
> He taught me the faithful Scriptures.
> He sent me to Rome to behold
> the Sovereign City
> and to see the Queen in golden raiment
> and golden shoes.
> There I saw a people who wear
> a splendid seal....
> I found brothers and sisters everywhere.
> Paul was my companion
> and everywhere faith led me.
> Everywhere it served me a fish from the spring,
> mighty and pure, whom a pure Virgin caught.

Without ceasing, she [the Church] gave fish
to friends to eat.
She has a delicious wine
which she gives with bread.[10]

What a fresh view of the Church! What wonder in the face of mystery! For Abercius the Church is a people who have baptism as their great seal, Christ as their shepherd, the faith and the Scriptures as their guide, the Eucharist (the freshwater fish) for food. The Church is to have brothers and sisters everywhere.

It was predicted at the beginning of the twentieth century that that would be the century of the Church, the century in which the Church would become newly aware of its importance after the long silence of the liberal enlightenment period. This certainly happened at the theological level. There were countless studies on the nature of the Church. Karl Barth called his theological system *Church Dogmatics*. The Second Vatican Council made the Church its central theme. There was also the *Ecclesiam suam* of Paul VI. But did love for the Church grow proportionately?

Sometimes it surprises us to discover that, throughout the patristic and medieval periods, we "do not have a single work that we can consider a study on the Church as such"[11] and that we had to wait until the Reformation to have a specific treatise, *De ecclesia*. But the reason is simple: There was no need to explain what was being lived. The fish does not need someone to explain to him what the sea is made of: It is immersed in it.

The saying is attributed to St. Ambrose, "The Church is beautiful in the souls." Whether it is his or not, the saying closely reflects the formula that is dear to him: *Ecclesia vel anima*, "the Church and the soul,"[12] which underlines the relationship between the two realities. The danger lies in looking for the Church in books or, worse, in newspapers, rather than in souls. In so doing one will never discover the Church's true mystery.

The Church's Crucial Ministry

The Church asks for our filial love and gratitude based on the fact that it is in the Church that we have the regenerative experience of being forgiven for our sins.

> It follows that apart from Christ the Church cannot grant forgiveness and that Christ has no will to forgive apart from the Church. The Church's authority to forgive extends only to the repentant, to those, that is, whom Christ has already touched; Christ, on his part, has no intention of regarding as forgiven one who despises the Church.[13]

As St. Ambrose notes, it is true that "in the remission of sins the Church develops a ministry. It does not exercise any power of its own since it is through the Holy Spirit that sins are forgiven."[14] But it is also true that it is a ministry desired by Christ. It therefore can have no substitute. In his autobiography the convert G. K. Chesterton wrote:

> When people ask me, or indeed anybody else, "Why did you join the Church of Rome?" the first essential answer, if it is partly an elliptical answer, is, "To get rid of my sins." For there is no other religious system that does *really* profess to get rid of people's sins.... I have only found one religion that dares to descend with me into the depth of myself.[15]

To the person who was pushing him to break with the institutional Church, asserting that it held him captive, Don Milani responded:

> We will not leave the Church because we cannot live without its sacraments and its teaching. . . . In this religion, among other very important and foundational things, is the sacrament of confession because of which, and almost for that reason alone, I am Catholic, in order to continually have the forgiveness of sins; to have it and to give it.[16]

The sacrament of reconciliation is the moment in which the greatest dignity of the individual believer is recognized. At every other moment in the life of the Church, the believer is one among many: one who hears the Word, one who receives the body of Christ. Here the believer is unique. At that moment the Church exists entirely and only for that person.

Moreover, the way in which one is cleansed of sin through confession is parallel to a natural and profound need of the human psyche, which is to be freed from what binds us by bringing it to light. The practice of psychoanalysis is based, in part, on this same principle, and sometimes people use it as a substitute for confession. There is a major difference, however: At the end of confession the priest gives you absolution, whereas at the end of a counseling session the psychoanalyst gives you a bill.

In order to become effective and resolute in the war against sin, our way of approaching this sacrament needs to be renewed "in the Spirit." This means living out confession not as a rite, habit, or imposition but as a personal encounter with the risen Christ. He allows us to touch his wounds, experiencing the healing power of his blood and "the joy of being saved."

Sometimes it is advisable to leave behind our usual way of examining our conscience (which has perhaps remained unchanged since childhood) and to go directly to the point. "What in me, Lord, has really displeased you since my last confession?" When I ask this question, I arrive at the answer almost immediately.

The gospel story that has accompanied us in this reflection ends with this bit of news: "And from that hour the disciple took her into his own home" (Jn 19:27). This passage also stands simultaneously for Mary and the Church. It is a new invitation to take the Church "with us" among the things that are most dear (*eis ta idia*). Lent is a time for conversion, and this year I have asked the Lord for the grace of conversion for the Church.

Let us end with the beautiful doxology from Ephesians 3:20-21:

> Now to him who by the power at work within us is able to accomplish abundantly far more than all we can ask or imagine, to him be glory in the church and in Christ Jesus to all generations, forever and ever. Amen.

CHAPTER FIVE

The Two Will Become One Flesh

The Family as Domestic Church

A careful reading of chapter five of the Letter to the Ephesians shows us that all of the sublime statements about the Church as the bride of Christ function as domestic moral teaching. At the theological level it is the *parenesis*, or exhortation, that comes down from the proclamation or *kerygma*. At the pastoral level, on the contrary, it is the proclamation that comes from the exhortation and creates this occasion. "Let the same mind be in you that was in Christ Jesus," said the apostle to the Philippians, and to reinforce this exhortation he made the wonderful proclamation of Christ we know:

> [T]hough he was in the form of God, [he] did not regard equality with God as something to be exploited, but emptied himself, taking the form of a slave, being born in human likeness.
>
> —PHILIPPIANS 2:6-7

Let us listen to the text that treats Christian domestic teaching:

> Be subject to one another out of reverence for Christ. Wives, be subject to your husbands as you are to the Lord. For the husband is the head of the wife just as Christ is the head of the church, the body of which he is the Savior. Just as the church is subject to Christ, so also wives ought to be, in everything, to their husbands. Husbands, love your wives, just as Christ loved the church and gave himself up for her.... In the same way, husbands should love their wives as they do their own bodies. He who loves his wife loves himself. For no one ever hates his own body, but he nourishes and tenderly cares for it, just as Christ does for the church, because we are members of his body. "For this

reason a man will leave his father and mother and be joined to his wife, and the two will become one flesh." This is a great mystery, and I am applying it to Christ and the church. Each of you, however, should love his wife as himself, and a wife should respect her husband.

—EPHESIANS 5:21-33

This text presents two fundamental relationships that together constitute the family: the husband-wife relationship and the parent-child relationship. Of the two the first is more important, because the second depends on it.

The Relationship between Husband and Wife

Reading the words of Paul with modern eyes, a problem soon arises. Paul entreats the husband "to love" his wife (and this is fine with us), but then he entreats the wife "to submit" to her husband. This seems unacceptable in a society that is firmly (and correctly) aware of the equality of the sexes.

In fact, it is true that on this point, St. Paul is at least partly conditioned by the mentality of his time. However, the solution is not to eliminate the word *submission* from the husband-wife relationship but rather to make it reciprocal, just as love must also be reciprocal. In other words, it is not only the husband who should love his wife but also the wife who should love her husband. Likewise, not only should the wife be submissive to her husband but also the husband to his wife. Reciprocal love and reciprocal submission: This is the exhortation with which our text began: "Be subject to one another out of reverence for Christ."

Submission is nothing but an aspect and a necessity of love. For the one who loves, being subject to the object of love is not humiliating but rather gladdening. In marriage submission indicates that one is taking account of the will of the spouse, of his or her opinion and intuition. It indicates that one is willing to dialogue rather than to make decisions on one's own, that one understands the necessity of sometimes renouncing his or her own point of view. In a word, it means remembering that one chose "to get married," that the spouses are literally under "the same yoke," (*coniugi*) freely joined.

St. John Chrysostom knew how to elicit the beautiful implications of the comparison between human marriage and the relationship between Christ and the Church. He directed these words to husbands:

> Do you want your wife to obey you like the Church obeys Christ? Then take care of her as Christ takes care of the Church…. Just as Christ did not threaten with cruelty nor by instilling fear or anything similar, but rather, with his great care, brought to his feet those who turned their backs…, conduct yourselves in this way towards your wives…. With fear you can bind a servant to you, but one's life companion, the mother of one's children, in whom is found every happiness, cannot be bound by using fear and threats but rather, with love and intimate affection. What kind of marriage would there be where a wife trembled before her husband? And what pleasure would the husband get from living with his wife if she were a slave rather than a free woman? [1]

The Image of God

In order to understand the beauty and dignity of the couple relationship, we must return to the Bible: "So God created humankind in his image, in the image of God he created them; male and female he created them" (Gn 1:27). As we can see, a relationship is established between beings created "in the image of God" and being "male and female." But what relationship can there be between these two things? In what sense are male and female—the human couple—an image of God? God is neither male nor female!

The likeness consists of this: God is one but is not alone. Love requires communion and interpersonal exchange; it asks that there be an "I" and a "you." For this reason the Christian God is one and triune. In God unity and distinction coexist: unity of nature—of willing, of intentions—and distinctions of characteristics and of persons.

Precisely in this the human couple is an image of God. The human family is a reflection of the Trinity. Husband and wife are truly one flesh, one heart, one soul, in spite of their differences of sex and personality. In the couple unity and diversity are reconciled. The spouses stand before one another as an "I" and a "you." They stand before the whole world, beginning with their children, as a "we," almost as if they were one person but plural. That is, "we," "your mother and I," "your father and I."

To the dignity and beauty that comes to marriage from creation is added that which comes from redemption—that is, from being a sign of the union between Christ and the Church. A married woman who is the mother of four children shows us how this relationship between Christ and the spouses truly illuminates, from the inside and in a profound way, the relationship between the married couple. She writes:

> On the cross Jesus said: "It is finished (consummated)." On the wedding night, it is also said of spouses, through the conjugal act, that they *consummate* their marriage in the Lord. (And everyone knows that this "passion" also consists of a type of death!) Every subsequent conjugal act between us is a celebration and deepening of that initial encounter, because it was there that we became one flesh. Jesus also gave his life once and for all, and every subsequent Eucharist makes present to us the unique event of Calvary.

We know well that this is the ideal and that reality is often very different: more humble and more complex and sometimes downright tragic. But we are so bombarded by negative cases of failure that perhaps, just once, it is not bad to resubmit the ideal of the couple, first at the simply natural, human level, then at the Christian level. It would be a problem if one were ashamed of the ideal because of a mistaken realism. That would signify the end of society. Young people have the right to have ideals passed on by adults, rather than just skepticism and cynicism. Nothing is more attractive than an ideal.

Fyodor Dostoyevsky offered a great description of conjugal love:

> And if once there has been love, if they have been married for love, why should love pass away? Surely one can keep it!… And if the husband is kind and straightforward, why should not love last? The first phase of married love will pass, it is true, but then there will come a love that is better still. Then there will be the union of souls, they will have everything in common, there will be no secrets between them. And once they have children, the most difficult times

will seem to them happy.... How can it fail to draw the father and mother nearer? People say that it's a trial to have children. Who says that? It is heavenly happiness!...You know—a little rosy baby boy at your bosom, and what husband's heart is not touched, seeing his wife nursing his child![2]

Parents and Children

The second relationship that constitutes the family is that of parents and children. Let us hear what our letter has to say in this regard:

> Children, obey your parents in the Lord, for this is right. "Honor your father and mother"—this is the first commandment with a promise: "so that it may be well with you and you may live long on the earth." And, fathers, do not provoke your children to anger, but bring them up in the discipline and instruction of the Lord.
>
> —EPHESIANS 6:1-4

Let us concentrate on the role of the father in his relationship with his children. That of the mother is usually less conflictual. Mothers are happy if we concentrate on the father-children relationship, as they are the first to suffer when there is a bad relationship between the two.

Who knows why literature, the arts, theater, and the media focus on only one human relationship: the sexual milieu between man and woman, between husband and wife. Maybe because it is so easy to talk about sex, dealing as it does with a disquieting reality. Humanity loves to fish in muddy waters. It would seem that there is nothing more than this to life. If an extraterrestrial were to happen upon our planet or were to see some of our television shows, he would find us ridiculous in our sexual obsession.

We leave almost unexplored another human relationship that is just as universal and vital, another great source of joy in life, the relationship of parent and child. Modern psychology has dealt with it a bit but usually only to highlight the parent-child conflict.

If instead one were to delve with serenity and objectivity into the heart of humankind, one would discover that a relationship with their children that works, which is intense and peaceful, for a mature adult is just as important and fulfilling as the relationship between man and woman. On the other hand, we also know how important this relationship is for the son or daughter. It leaves a tremendous void when it is missing.

According to Scripture, just as the man-woman relationship has as its model the Christ-Church relationship, so the parent-child relationship has as its model the relationship between God the Father and Jesus. St. Paul says that it is from God the Father that "every family in heaven and on earth takes its name" (Eph 3:15), which is to say that God is the one from whom every paternity gets its existence, meaning, and value.

Just as cancer usually attacks the most delicate organs in men and women, so, too, does the destructive power of sin attack the most vital ganglions of human existence. There is nothing more vulnerable to abuse, to being taken advantage of, to violence, than the man-woman relationship, and there is nothing more vulnerable to deformation than the parent-child relationship, which can be tainted by authoritarianism, paternalism, rebellion, rejection, and lack of communication.

Psychoanalysis believes that deep down in the unconscious of every son the so-called Oedipus complex—that is, the secret desire to kill the father. Without bothering with Freud's psychoanalysis, the news takes it upon itself to place such terrible facts before our eyes on a daily basis. This is typically diabolical work. One of the original meanings of the word *devil* was, "the one who divides, who separates." He is not satisfied with putting one social class against another, nor even with setting one gender against the other. He wants to strike deeper, to set parents against their children and children against their parents.

The devil often succeeds. He poisons one of the greatest sources of joy in human life and one of the most important factors in the growth and maturation process of the human person. The suffering is reciprocal. There are parents whose most profound suffering in life is to be rejected and even despised by their children, for whom they have done everything they could. And there are children who likewise suffer misunderstanding and rejection by their parents. Some have even been told by their fathers in moments of rage, "You are not my child."

What can be done to neutralize this satanic work in our society? When John the Baptist was born, the angel said that one of his tasks was "to turn the hearts of parents to their children" (Lk 1:17). This echoes Malachi 4:6, which also includes "the hearts of children to their parents." It is important that this task of the precursor be continued. We need to launch a great initiative of reconciliation, of healing in the relationships between parents and children. We must unmask the work of Satan.

Imitate the Father

What to do? First of all believe. Regain a sense of trust in parenthood as much more than a biological role. It is a mystery and a sharing in God's own parenthood. Ask God for the gift of parenthood, of knowing what it is to be a parent. Ask this of the Holy Spirit.

Then make the effort to imitate the heavenly Father. The Letter to the Ephesians suggests that children be obedient, but what does it recommend to parents? That they not "provoke" their children (see also Col 3:21). Stated positively, this means having patience with them, being understanding, not expecting everything at once, knowing how to wait for them to mature, knowing how to forgive mistakes. It means not discouraging them with continual rebukes and negative observations but rather encouraging every small effort. This means communicating a sense of freedom, protection, self-trust and security, just as God is "our refuge and strength, a very present help in trouble" (Psalm 46).

To any parent who wants to know what not to do, I would suggest the famous *Letter to His Father* by Franz Kafka. Kafka's father wanted to know why the son was afraid of him, and the writer responded with a letter intertwining love and sadness. He reproved his father above all for never realizing the tremendous power he had over him, both good and bad. The father's peremptory "And not a word of contradiction!" had inhibited the son to the extent that he almost forgot how to speak. When he would bring home from school some joy, a child's deed or a good grade the reaction was always the same: "I have other things to think about." (The "other things" was his business.) One can read between the lines what he could have been: a friend to his son, a confidant, a role model, his entire world.[3]

Do not be afraid of literally imitating God the Father and saying to your own son or daughter, if circumstances call for it: "You are my beloved son! You are my beloved daughter in whom I am well pleased!" In other words, "I am proud of you, of being your parent!" If these words come from the heart and at the right moment, they can produce miracles and can give wings to the heart of the boy or girl. For the parent it is like generating his or her own child a second time and with greater awareness.

One thing above all is necessary in our imitation of God, who "sends rain on the righteous and on the unrighteous" (Mt 5:45). God wants us to be better than we are, much better, but he accepts and loves us as we are. He loves us in hope. Even an earthly father (and here the discourse is valid even for mothers) should not love just the ideal child, the one longed for: brilliant in school, educated, successful in everything. The parent should love the real child whom God has given, cherishing that person for who he or she is. How many frustrations could be resolved by serenely accepting the will of God with regard to one's children, while making every possible formative effort on their behalf.

Draw Strength from the Lord

The Word of God does not simply suggest to spouses and Christian parents the duties they are to fulfill; it also communicates the grace that gives the strength to accomplish those duties. What new thing does grace bring to the human ideal of marriage? Simple: the possibility of changing, of becoming, of reaching the ideal for which one longs. Of course, this does not occur automatically and magically but with the right collaboration, through a path of learning and growth.

The sacrament of marriage grants the spouses the "grace of this state." Grace is that "something more" that comes from the cross of Christ, which does not destroy or supplant nature but lifts it up, heals and fortifies it and gives new reason to overcome difficulties. It redeems us from every failure.

The following praise of conjugal happiness can help us measure what grace adds to nature:

> How shall we ever be able adequately to describe the happiness of that marriage which the Church arranges, the Sacrifice strengthens, upon which the blessing sets a seal, at which angels are present as witnesses, and to which the Father gives His consent? How beautiful, then, the marriage of two Christians, two who are one in hope, one in desire, one in the way of life they follow, one in the religion they practice. They are as brother and sister, both servants of the same Master. Nothing divides them, either in flesh or in spirit. They are, in very truth, two in one flesh; and where there is but one flesh there is also but one spirit. They pray together, instruct one another, encourage one another and strengthen one another. Together they visit God's church and partake of God's Banquet; together they face difficulties and persecution, and share their joys. They have no secrets from one another; they never shun each other's company; they never bring sorrow to each other's hearts.... They need not be shy about making the Sign of the Cross.... Hearing and seeing this, Christ rejoices. To these he gives his peace. Where there are two together, there he is also present; and where he is, evil is not.[4]

The grace of marriage is identified with the Holy Spirit,

who is the "gift" or, better, God's "self-giving." When a married couple is open to the action of the Holy Spirit, he communicates to them what he is. He infects them, so to speak, renewing in them the capacity and joy of giving themselves to one another. The sign that something is changing in the relationship between two spouses, that grace is working above nature, the *agape* over *eros*, is when each stops asking, "What else could my spouse do for me which she, or he, does not?" and begins asking, "What more can I do for my spouse which I still do not do for her, or for him?"

In this way marriage is sanctified, not through something that comes from the outside—through the rite that is celebrated or the holy water sprinkled on the rings—but in itself, in the most intimate gesture. One is no longer compelled to live the moment of intimacy as separate, as if to hide it from God, but on the contrary, as a moment that is strengthened by the presence of God among them and by God's love for them. In the act of giving oneself to the other, the spouses are truly "the image of God," because they reflect the fruitful love that is in the Trinity.

Grace needs to be cultivated; for this reason the *paranesis* of the Letter to the Ephesians ends by indicating the means for living the highest ideal of Christian life in the family:

> Finally, be strong in the Lord and in the strength of his power.... Take the helmet of salvation, and the sword of the Spirit, which is the word of God. Pray in the Spirit at all times in every prayer and supplication.

> —EPHESIANS 6:10, 17-18

It is at the moment in which they pray together or listen to and comment on the Word of God that the family appears most clearly as the "domestic church."

Notes

CHAPTER ONE: "THROUGH HIM THE WHOLE STRUCTURE IS HELD TOGETHER"

1. Pope John Paul II, *Novo millennio ineunte*, n. 42.

2. Rudolf Schnackenburg, *Der Brief an die Ephesians eser*, Zurich 1982, 359.

3. See. H. U. von Balthasar, "*Casta meretrix*," in "*Sponsa Verbi. Skizzen zur Theologie*," II, Einsiedeln 1961.

4. St. Gregory the Great, *Morals on the Book of Job* (London: Rivington, 1844), Vol. 1, Book XX, 446.

5. I have dealt more extensively with the problem of Christian-Jewish relationships in a Good Friday sermon in St. Peter's Basilica; to it I refer the reader to complete what I am saying in this occasion: http://www.cantalamessa.org/en/1998venerdi.htm.

6. Eugene Fisher, "Why Convert the Saved?" in *The Tablet*, July 14, 2001.

7. Fisher. The same idea can be found in a document coming from the joint Catholic-Jewish commission of the United States (not signed by the bishops but rather their delegates): *Reflections on Covenant and Mission. Consultation of the National Council of Synagogues and Bishops' Committee for Ecumenical and Interreligious Affairs*, August 12, 2002.

8. Rosalind Moss, "O Jerusalem, Jerusalem.… From the Heart of a Jewish Convert: An Open Letter to William Cardinal Keeler in Response to 'Reflections on Covenant and Mission'" in *Remnant of Israel: New Hope, Kentucky 40052*.

9. Hermas's *The Shepherd* enjoyed a respect close to that of Scripture among some early Christians. The vision mentioned here is of an aged woman, representing the Church, who shows the shepherd a tower being built on the water. He asks, "Why on water?" and she responds, "Your life was saved through the seal of water, and shall be saved hereafter through water; and the tower has been founded by the utterance of the glorious Name and is maintained by the unseen power of the Master." (Jardine Williams, trans., *Shepherd of Hermas: The Gentle Apocalypse* [Redwood City, Calif.: Proteus Publishing, 1992], 37).

CHAPTER TWO: THERE IS ONE BODY, ONE SPIRIT

1. From the Eucharistic Prayer for Masses for Various Needs and Occasions.

2. Clement, "The Letter of the Church of Rome to the Church of Corinth, Commonly Called Clement's First Letter," 46:5-7, in Cyril R. Richardson, ed., *Early Christian Fathers* (New York: Macmillan, 1970), 65. An allusion to Ephesians 1:18 is also found in 59:3 of the letter (Richardson, 70). Thus the letter was already known in Rome before the end of the century, a sign that, if not written by Paul himself, it must have been written not long after his death.

3. See Heinrich Schlier, "*Der Brief an die Epheser. Ein Kommentar,*" (Dusseldorf: Patmos Verlag, 1962), ad loc.

4. *Novo millennio ineunte*, n. 42.

5. *Novo millennio ineunte*, n. 44.

6. Augustine, "Sermon 267" in John E. Rotelle, ed. *The Works of Saint Augustine: Sermons*, Edmund Hill, trans. (New Rochelle, N.Y.: New City, 1993), III/7, 276.

7. Thomas Aquinas, *Commentary on the Letter to the Romans*, V, 1, n. 392.

8.   See St. Augustine, "Treatise on the Gospel of John," in Philip Schaff, ed., *Augustine: Homilies on the Gospel of John, Homilies on the First Epistle of John, Soliloquies, Vol. 7 of Nicene and Post-Nicene Fathers* (Peabody, Mass.: Hendrickson, 1995), 195. For Latin original see Augustine, *Treatise on the Gospel of John*, 32, 8 (PL 35, 1646).

9.   St. Augustine, "Sermon 269," in *Rotelle*, 286. For Latin original see Augustine, *Discourses*, 269, 4 (PL 38, 1236 s).

10. Clement here alludes to a number of Scripture passages. See Is 13:11; Ps 33:10; Jb 5:11; 1 Sm 2:7; Dt 32:39.

11. Clement, 59-61, in Richardson, 71-72.

CHAPTER THREE: CHRIST LOVED THE CHURCH

1.   Plato refers to ancient marriage customs in his Book VI, 774e-775a. See *The Laws of Plato*, A. E. Taylor, trans. (London: Dent & Sons, 1934), 157-158. See also O. Casel., "*Le bain nuptial de l'Eglise*" in *Dieu Vivant* 4 (1945), 43-49.

2.   Paschal Homily attributed to Hippolytus, 53 (SCh 27, 181).

3.   John Chrysostom, *Baptismal Instructions*, Paul W. Harkins, trans. (London: Newman, 1963), 62; see Augustine, *Treatise on the Gospel of John*, tractate 120, no. 2 in Schaff, 434-435.

4.   J. W. Goethe, *Faust*, Martin Greenberg, tr. (New Haven and London: Yale University Press, 1998), 245. Original German: "*Alles Vergängliche/ Ist nur ein Gleichnis; / Das Unzulängliche, / Hier wird's Ereignis,*" *Goethe's Faust* (Hamburg: Christian Wegner Verlag, 1966), 364.

5.   See Cyril of Jerusalem, "Mystogogical Lecture IV," no. 3 in Leo P. McCauley and Anthony A. Stephenson, trans., *The Works of Cyril of Jerusalem*, vol. 2, vol. 64 of *The Fathers of the Church* (Washington, D.C.: Catholic University of America Press, 1970), 181-182.

6.   Elizabeth of the Trinity, *Letters*, 261 to her mother (in *Opere*, Rome 1967, 457): the context is interesting: "The bride belongs to the groom. Mine has taken me. He desires that I be an additional humanity for him."

7.   Schlier, quoted, ad loc.

8. Catherine of Sienna, "Prayer 13" (Rome, February 18, 1379) as quoted in Giuliana Cavallini, *Catherine of Siena* (New York: Geoffrey Chapman, 1998), 43-44. Also see Suzanne Noffke, ed., *The Prayers of Catherine of Siena* (New York: Paulist, 1983), 112-113.

9. Erasmus of Rotterdam, *Hyperaspistae Book 1*, in Charles Trinkaus, ed., *Collected Works of Erasmus*, Peter Macardle and Clarence H. Miller, trans. (Toronto: University of Toronto Press, 1999), 117. *Opere omnia*, X, Leida 1706, col. 1258: "*Fero igtur hanc Ecclesiam, donec videro meliorem; et eadem me ferre cogitur, donec ipse fiam melior.*"

10. Antoine de Saint-Exupéry, *Flight to Arras* (translation of *Pilote de Guerre*), Lewis Galantiére, trans. (New York: Reynal & Hitchcock, 1942), 222-223.

11. Translators' note: This translation of Job is our own, because the *NRSV* translation does not render the Italian used by the author. The *NRSV* translation is: "See, he will kill me; I have no hope; but I will defend my ways to his face" (Jb 13:15).

12. Pascal, Blaise, *Pensées*, 471, in *The Provincial Letters*, Pensées, Scientific Treatises, W.F. Trotter, trans. (Chicago: Encyclopedia Britannica, 1952), 256; see also the biography written by his sister Gilberte Perier: *La vie de Monsieur Pascal in: Pascal, Ouvres complètes*, Paris 1954, S. 26-27.

13. Translators' note: This translation of Ephesians is our own, because the *NRSV* translation does not render the translation used by the author. The *NRSV* translation is "As shoes for your feet put on whatever will make you ready to proclaim the gospel of peace" (Eph 6:15).

14. Ignatius of Antioch, *Letter to the Romans*, inscription. This is alternately translated "holding the chief place in love."

15. Bernard of Clairvaux, *De consideratione*, Book 4, chapter 4, no. 12 in *Five Books On Consideration: Advice to a Pope*, John D. Anderson and Elizabeth T. Kennan, trans., Vol. 13 of *The Works of Bernard of Clairvaux* (Kalamazoo, Mich.: Cistercian, 1976), 123-124, 125.

16. Catherine of Siena, "Letter 373," to Blessed Raymond of Capua, as quoted in Michael de la Bedoyere, *Catherine: Saint of Siena* (London: Hollis & Carter, 1947), 225.

17. Catherine of Siena, "Letter 302," to Urban VI.

18. Catherine of Siena, "Letter 371" in de la Bedoyere, 226.

19. This is our translation of the Italian. Catherine of Siena, *Epistola* 371.

20. Catherine of Siena, "Prayer 14" (Rome, February 20, 1379), in Noffke, 119.

CHAPTER FOUR: "SON, BEHOLD YOUR MOTHER!"

1. *Theodore of Mopsuestia on the Minor Epistles of St. Paul*, H.B. Swete, ed. (Cambridge: Cambridge University Press, 1880), 123.

2. Pope John Paul II, *Redemptoris mater* ("Mother of the Redeemer"), n. 47, quoting *Lumen gentium*, n. 65.

3. *Lumen gentium*, n. 61.

4. St. Francis of Assisi, "A salutation of the Blessed Virgin Mary," in *Francis of Assisi, Early Documents*, vol. I (New York: New City Press, 1999), 163.

5. Augustine, "Sermon 213," in Rotelle, III/6, 145.

6. Isaac of Stella, "Sermon 31" (PL 194, 1863) in Isaac of Stella, *Sermons on the Christian Year*, Vol. 2, Hugh McCaffery, trans. (Kalamazoo, Mich.: Cistercian, 1979); see *Lumen gentium*, n. 64.

7. Clement of Alexandria, *The Instructor*, Book I, chapter 6, in William Wilson, trans., *The Writings of Clement of Alexandria*, Vol. IV of Alexander Roberts and James Donaldson, eds., *Ante-Nicene Christian Library: Translations of the Writings of the Fathers* (Edinburgh: Clark, 1947), 142.

8. St. Cyprian, *The Unity of the Catholic Church*, Maurice Bévenot, trans. (Westminster, Md.: Newman, 1957), 48-49.

9. Psalm 45:13. See Jerome, *Letters*, 107, 7. See also Augustine, *Expositions on the Book of Psalms*, Psalm 45, section 24 in Philip Schaff, ed., *Augustin: Expositions on the Book of Psalms*, vol. 8 of *Nicene and Post-Nicene Fathers* (Peabody, Mass.: Hendrickson, 1995), 153.

10. Greek original with Latin translation in *Enchiridion Fontium Historiae Ecclesiasticae Antiquae* (Barcelona: Herder, 1965), n. 155, 94. Abercius saw the Roman community as "the queen dressed in gold" of Psalm 45!

11. L. Bouyer, *L'Eglise de Dieu* (Paris: du Cerf, 1970) chap. 1.

12. St. Ambrose, *On the Psalm CXVIII*, 6,18 (CSEL 62, p. 117); see Origen, *On the Canticle III* (GCS 33, pp. 185 and 190).

13. Isaac of Stella, "Sermon 11," (PL 194, 1729) in Isaac of Stella, *Sermons on the Christian Year*, Vol. 1, Hugh McCaffery, trans. (Kalamazoo, Mich.: Cistercian, 1979), 96.

14. St. Ambrose, *On the Holy Spirit*, III, 137.

15. G. K. Chesterton, *Autobiography* (London: Hutchinson, 1969), 329, 341.

16. See M. Lancisi, *Il segreto di Don Milani* (Casale Monferrato 2002), 98.

CHAPTER FIVE: THE TWO WILL BECOME ONE FLESH

1. John Chrysostom, *On the Letter to the Ephesians*, Homily 20 (PG 62, 137). Translators' version.

2. Fyodor Dostoevsky, *Notes from the Underground*, in *The Short Novels of Dostoevsky* (New York: Dial, 1945), 197.

3. See Franz Kafka, *Letter to His Father*, Ernst Kaiser and Eithne Wilkins, trans. (New York: Schocken, 1966), 7, 21, 35.

4. Tertullian, *To His Wife*, Book 2, 6-9. See also Vol. 4 of *Ante-Nicene Fathers*, Alexander Roberts and James Donaldson, eds. (Peabody, Mass.: Hendrickson, 1995), 48.